BRADFORD BUSES

KEITH A. JENKINSON

AMBERLEY

First published 2017

Amberley Publishing
The Hill, Stroud
Gloucestershire, GL5 4EP

www.amberley-books.com

Copyright © Keith A. Jenkinson, 2017

The right of Keith A. Jenkinson to be identified as the Author of this work has been asserted in accordance with the Copyright, Designs and Patents Act 1988.

ISBN 978 1 4456 7478 0 (print)
ISBN 978 1 4456 7479 7 (ebook)

All rights reserved. No part of this book may be reprinted or reproduced or utilised in any form or by any electronic, mechanical or other means, now known or hereafter invented, including photocopying and recording, or in any information storage or retrieval system, without the permission in writing from the Publishers.

British Library Cataloguing in Publication Data.
A catalogue record for this book is available from the British Library.

Typesetting by Amberley Publishing.
Printed in the UK.

Introduction

Originally a rural market town located in the Aire Valley of the West Riding of Yorkshire some 8.6 miles west of Leeds, Bradford gradually developed to become a municipal borough in 1847 and three years later its population had grown to 182,000. Although Bradford had iron, sandstone and coal industries, its meteoric rise was largely due to the woollen textile industry, which had developed in the early years of the nineteenth century and became known worldwide for its quality. In 1897, the municipal borough was granted city status.

Transport first reached Bradford in the form of railways, with the Leeds & Bradford Railway opening a station in Forster Square on 1 July 1846, the Lancashire & Yorkshire Railway (L&YR) opening one at Drake Street on 9 May 1850 and the Great Northern Railway (GNR) commencing operation from Adolphus Street in 1854. Joint co-operation, however, saw the L&YR and GNR relocate to a new station known as the Exchange in 1867. This remained in use until 1962 when it was relocated to a new site and, together with a new bus station, was renamed the Interchange.

Meanwhile, after the old mail coaches had succumbed to the railways, public road transport first appeared on 2 February 1882 when the privately owned Bradford Tramways Company began a horse tram service from Rawson Square to Lister Park. Following this, steam-hauled trams were introduced along Leeds Road five months later on 3 August and thereafter both forms of traction were expanded to other parts of Bradford before being ultimately taken over by Bradford Corporation in 1898. Immediately, work began on the electrification of the tramway and the last horse-drawn and steam-hauled trams operated their final journeys on 31 January 1902 and 1 April 1903 respectively, with the new electric trams continuing to serve the city until 6 May 1950. During this period, a tramway service had been opened on 7 June 1909 between Bradford and Leeds, which was jointly operated by both municipalities; but with Leeds operating on standard gauge track and Bradford on narrower 4-foot-wide lines, it was necessary to taper the track between the two gauges where they connected at Stanningley and use trams with specially designed axles, upon which the wheels could move to adjust to the taper. Although successful, the through service was discontinued on 31 March 1918 due to financial reasons and thereafter passengers had to transfer between trams at Stanningley to be able to complete their journey.

Looking to the future during the early part of the twentieth century, both Bradford and Leeds Corporation introduced trolleybuses to their cities on 20 June 1911, being the first in the UK to do so, and while Leeds abandoned its tiny system in 1928,

Bradford's grew dramatically and continued until 26 March 1972, when it gained the distinction of being the last UK trolleybus operator.

Although motorbuses in independent ownership had appeared in Bradford from around the turn of the century, it was not, however, until 13 May 1926 that they were operated by the municipality, when it began competing with local, privately owned Blythe & Berwick on a service between Lister Park and Bankfoot. Following its success, the Corporation introduced numerous new services to areas not served by its trams and trolleybuses and quickly became the main provider of public transport within the city boundary. Independent operators still continued to maintain services into Bradford from areas outside the city, albeit with numerous restrictions relating to the picking up and setting down of passengers and protective fares, etc.

Until the mid-1920s Bradford had no bus station as such and all the services running into the city used stops located on the city's streets, but then Blythe & Berwick took the lease of a plot of land in Chester Street, which was over the next ten years developed into a terminal that was used by West Yorkshire Road Car Co., Hebble Motor Services, Yorkshire Woollen District, North Western, Sheffield Joint Omnibus Committee, Ribble and Samuel Ledgard. This remained in use until 1977, when it was replaced by the new Interchange, which was built between Nelson Street and Bridge Street and incorporated the old, albeit slightly relocated, Exchange railway station. Beneath the Interchange was a new bus garage for West Yorkshire PTE, which had been formed on 1 April 1974 by the merging of the Bradford, Halifax, Huddersfield and Leeds municipal bus undertakings and introduced a new corporate identity and livery. As a consequence, six of Bradford City Transport's seven bus depots were closed and their operations moved to the new Hall Ings (Interchange) base. Then, in July 1981, the West Yorkshire PTE and the National Bus Company formed a new company – Metro National Transport Company – in order to co-ordinate all the bus and rail services in West Yorkshire, and to this end all the NBC companies operating within the PTE area were required to paint their vehicles in corporate PTE livery and display MetroBus fleet names, although in the event this was never completed before the deregulation of local bus services occurred on 26 October 1986.

Unlike many other towns and cities, Bradford suffered little from new operators who attempted to compete with the established companies who maintained services within and from outside the city following deregulation, and although a few newcomers made brave attempts and successfully gained some tendered services, these were mostly short-lived and soon disappeared. In the meantime, however, West Yorkshire PTE formed an arms-length company under the title of Yorkshire Rider in 1986, but two years later, on 21 October 1988, sold it to its employees, who in August 1989 purchased the Bradford, Leeds and Otley operations (and vehicles) of West Yorkshire Road Car Co. Then, on 15 April 1994, Yorkshire Rider was sold to Badgerline, who on 16 June 1995 merged with the GRT Group to form First Bus, who is today the main provider of Branford's city bus services while Arriva and Transdev Keighley maintain most of those operating beyond the city boundary. Following the recent demise of Geldards of Leeds and the Brighouse-based Ladies Only Travel, local independent TLC Travel, who maintain a number of tendered services in and around the city, is the only significant independent to be seen in Bradford, although Transdev Keighley Bus Company has recently attempted to gain a foothold within the tendered market.

Despite Bradford's Interchange being the main transport hub, a small number of cross-city services continue to use street bus stops rather than visit the terminal, where all the different operators can be seen and photography is easily achieved opposite its two entrances and exits.

Although the majority of the photographs within this book have been taken by myself, without the generous help of others there would have been several gaps and as such I thank all those who have helped. While I have credited these where known within the captions, I have unfortunately been unable to establish the origins of several views purchased at various enthusiast gatherings, etc. To those photographers I offer my sincere apologies and hope that they will forgive me and gain pleasure in seeing their work in print as their contributions have been of immense value in portraying the pictorial history of Bradford's buses over half a century.

Keith A. Jenkinson
Queensbury, 2017

With five trolleybuses in sight on Market Street, collecting its Wibsey-bound passengers is Bradford City Transport Karrier W4 No. 718 (DKY 718), which carried a Park Royal body when new in 1945 and was given its East Lancs body in 1957. (Derek Yates collection)

Lined up in Leeds Road, Thornbury, on 24 March 1972 ready to depart on a tour on the final day of public operation, are four East Lancs-rebodied trolleybuses headed by Sunbeam F4 No. 843 (FWX 913), which began life in 1948 as a Brush-bodied single-decker of Mexborough & Swinton, receiving its new body in December 1962. Behind it is Karrier W4 No. 712 (DKY 712), which was new to Bradford City Transport in 1945 with Park Royal bodywork.

Seen here on 26 March 1972, decorated for the trolleybus system's final closing ceremony, is Sunbeam F4 No. 844 (FWX 914), which was new as a single-decker with Mexborough & Swinton and was acquired in 1961 by Bradford City Transport, who gave it its new East Lancs body in December of the following year. (Derek Yates collection)

Standing in the yard of the bleakly located Horton Bank Top former tram depot on 28 November 1966, is Bradford City Transport's elegant Weymann-bodied AEC Regent III No. 38 (FKY 38).

Entering Leeds Road from Forster Square on a journey to Stanningley is Bradford City Transport's all-Leyland PD2/1 No. 572 (EKY 572). (Derek Yates collection)

New to Bradford City Transport in December 1962 and seen here in preservation is East Lancs-bodied AEC Regent III No. 82 (HKW 82).

Bradford Buses

One of only twelve single-deckers in Bradford City Transport's fleet, dual-door Marshall-bodied AEC Swift No. 503 (NAK 503H) is pictured here at the foot of Sunbridge Road in 1971. (Derek Yates collection)

In 1958 Bradford City Transport purchased twenty-five former London Transport RT-type AEC Regent IIIRTs. Retaining its roof route number box, now preserved No. 410 (HLW 159) is a reminder of the buses that served the city admirably for several years. (Author's collection)

The last bus to be purchased new by Bradford City Transport was Alexander-bodied Daimler CRL6 No. 355 (XAK 355L), which joined the fleet in August 1972 and is seen on a former trolleybus route at Lidget Green on 30 March 1973.

Seen in 1964 at the Queensbury terminus of the services to Bradford and Halifax before they were joined together are Bradford City Transport's Weymann-bodied AEC Regent III No. 14 (FKY 14) and Halifax Joint Omnibus Committee's MCCW-bodied AEC Regent V No. 217 (LJX 217). (David Hudson collection)

Pictured here after being preserved and wearing the livery of its original owner, front entrance Roe-bodied Daimler CVG6LX No. 574 (574 CMW) was purchased new by Leeds City Transport for the Leeds–Bradford 72 service, which was jointly operated with Bradford City Transport. (Author's collection)

Standing in Chester Street bus station on 27 October 1967 is West Yorkshire Road Car Co.'s ex-Ledgard, Roe-bodied AEC Regent V No. DAW5 (1949 U) on an enthusiast tour and Bradford City Transport's MCCW-bodied AEC Regent V No. 129 (YAK 129), which is operating the former Ledgard service to Leeds. (Neil Halliday)

Seen in Bradford city centre, Huddersfield Corporation's East Lancs-bodied Daimler CVG6LX No. 465 (HVH 465D) awaits departure to its home town on route 64, while behind it is a Bradford City Transport's Alexander-bodied Daimler CRG6LX and about to overtake is West Riding Roe-bodied Guy Wulfrunian No. 1023 (BHL 374C). (Neil Halliday)

Awaiting disposal at Bradford depot in March 1968, with green paint covering the cream area of its livery, is West Yorkshire Road Car Co.'s ECW-bodied Bristol KSW6B No. DBW27 (LWR 413), while alongside it is ECW-bodied Bristol LS6G No. CUG9 (LYG 715).

Hiding behind Hebble's NCME-bodied AEC Regent V No. 618 (PCP 404) and one of their Harrington-bodied AEC Reliances in Chester Street bus station is a North Western Bristol RELL, awaiting its departure to Manchester. (Barry Newsome collection)

Pictured at Queensbury while being demonstrated to Hebble in 1963 is Park Royal-bodied AEC Renown 7552 MX. (Barry Newsome collection)

Seen in Chester Street bus station on the TransPennine service to Manchester is Yorkshire Woollen District Leyland Olympic No. 730 (HD 9130). (Barry Newsome collection)

Seen on 21 July 1966 close to the home of its owner, Johnson of Wyke, Roe-bodied AEC Regent III BCP No. 537 still wears the livery of its former owner, the Halifax Corporation.

Smith's Glen Coaches', Shipley, VHE No. 191 began life with Yorkshire Traction in 1950 as a Windover-bodied Leyland PS2/3 coach and was given its new Roe body by its Barnsley-based owners in 1961. (Neil Halliday)

Immaculately presented and seen here while owned by Bradford coach operator Norman Boyes is ex-Yorkshire Woollen District MCCW-bodied Leyland PD3A/1 GHD No. 765. After later spending time in preservation, it ended up in Poland as a fast food outlet.

West Riding frequently operated its Roe-bodied Guy Wulfrunians, like No. 906 (THL 906), into Bradford.

Parked opposite Samuel Ledgard's Bradford depot are ex-Bristol Omnibus Co.'s 1948 vintage BBW-bodied Leyland PD1A (LAE 2) and all-Leyland PD2/1 (MUA 862), which was purchased new in 1949. (David Hudson collection)

Following Samuel Ledgard's all-Leyland PD2/12 PNW 92 along Galloway Lane, Pudsey, on its way from Bradford to Leeds on 14 October 1967, is one of the company's ex-London Transport AEC Regent IIIRTs.

Resting at the Calverley terminus of the service to Acres Hall on 14 October 1967 – the last day of Ledgard's operation before its sale to West Yorkshire Road Car Co. – is former London Transport AEC Regent IIIRT KGK 687.

Awaiting disposal at West Yorkshire Road Car Co.'s Bradford depot on 7 May 1968 are former Ledgard ex-Ribble Burlingham lowbridge-rebodied Leyland PD1A BCK 441, an all-Leyland PD1 and ex-London RT OLD 705.

Seen in Chester Street bus station in 1968 with a West Yorkshire Road Car Co.'s ECW-bodied Bristol MW6G coach is ECW-bodied Bristol KSW6B No. DBW21 (KWU 377), which was retrofitted with rear platform doors and retains its original destination layout. (John Howie)

Having had its front destination screen modified to eliminate the intermediate display, West Yorkshire Road Car Co.'s ECW-bodied Bristol LL5G No. SGL16 (JWU 886) rests in Chester Street bus station together with one of the company's Bristol FS6Bs, a Ledgard ex-Rochdale AEC Regent III and a Hebble AEC Regent V.

Typifying West Yorkshire Road Car Co.'s large fleet of Bristol Lodekkas is FS6B No. DX180 (DWU 679B), which is seen here in its original Tilling-style red and cream livery. (Neil Halliday)

Devoid of a fleet name, West Yorkshire Road Car Co.'s ECW-bodied Bristol VRT No. VR13 (XWX 58G) is seen here in Bradford while operating the former Hebble service to Huddersfield. (Neil Halliday)

On loan to West Yorkshire Road Car Co. from East Yorkshire Motor Services' Scarborough & District subsidiary, Leyland National No. 132 (SGR 132R), which began life with United Automobile Services, heads up Bolton Road, Bradford, on a 670 journey to Leeds.

Bradford Buses 21

Seen after overturning on Manningham Lane at the bottom of Oak Lane on 20 July 1967 is West Yorkshire Road Car Co.'s Bristol LD6B Lodekka No. DX18 (OWX 162), which was ultimately repaired and returned to service.

Making its way along Canal Road en route to Bradford Interchange is West Yorkshire Robin Hood-bodied Iveco 49.10 No. 176 (E341 SWY) adorned with Shipley Hoppa branding.

Sandwiched between West Yorkshire PTE's former Bradford City Transport MCCW-bodied AEC Regent Vs No. 2182 (2182 KW) and No. 2188 (2188 KW) in the yard of Ludlam Street depot, Bradford, are ex-Huddersfield Corporation's Roe-bodied Leyland PD3A/2s No. 414 (WVH 414) and No. 418 (WVH 418), which were both being operated in Bradford. (Author's collection)

Painted in West Yorkshire PTE's MetroBus livery is Plaxton Derwent-bodied Leyland Leopard No. 8534 (RWU 534R), which is seen here in preservation in April 2017. (Martin Counter)

Wearing MetroBus livery and collecting its passengers in Bradford city centre in 1981 is West Yorkshire PTE's MCW Scania Metropolitan No. 2647 (MNW 647P). (F.W. York)

Passing through Clayton Heights while on test on 26 March 1980 before entering revenue-earning service is West Yorkshire PTE's brand-new MCW Metrobus No. 7502 (JUM 502V).

Yorkshire Rider's ex-West Yorkshire Road Car Co. ECW-bodied Leyland Olympian No. 5518 (B518 UWW) is seen heading to Bradford, still wearing its former owner's Yorkshire Coastliner livery.

Branded for the Bradford and Leeds to Sheffield White Rose express services and displaying Gold Rider fleet names, Yorkshire Rider's Optare-bodied Leyland Olympian No. 5511 (C511 KBT) awaits its passengers in Bradford Interchange.

Bradford Buses

Seen at Bradford Interchange in 1986 on the Bradford Shop Hopper service is West Yorkshire PTE's (almost new) coach-seated, Optare-bodied Leyland Cub No. 1802 (C802 KBT). (Author's collection)

Hired by West Yorkshire PTE from South Yorkshire PTE, Optare-bodied Dennis Domino No. 54 (C54 HDT) collects its passengers at Bradford Interchange's car park terminus of the 700 Shop Hopper service on 17 September 1987.

Wearing a branded livery for Bradford's Shop Hopper service, on which the fare then was 5p, West Yorkshire PTE's Optare-bodied Leyland Cub No. 1810 (C810 KBT) is seen here at Bradford Interchange car park while a PTE Leyland Olympian passes above on its way into the bus station.

Painted in corporate West Yorkshire PTE livery and displaying MetroBus fleet names at Bradford Interchange is Yorkshire Woollen District's Leyland National No. 158 (TUG 806R).

The last Bradford bus to wear West Yorkshire PTE Verona green and cream livery, Roe-bodied Leyland AN68/1R No. 6020 (GUG 547N), with Yorkshire Rider vinyls covering its former MetroBus fleet name, climbs Bridge Street on 6 August 1990. When new in 1974 it was exhibited at the Commercial Motor Show at Earls Court, London.

Adorned with an all-over advertising livery, Yorkshire Rider's Optare Star Rider-bodied Mercedes-Benz 811D No. 2002 (E202 PWY) is seen at the Bradford Interchange car park terminus of the city's Shop Hopper 700 service.

Still wearing its West Yorkshire Road Car Co. livery, albeit now with Yorkshire Rider fleet names, Robin Hood-bodied Iveco 49.10 No. 2062 (D551 HNW) descends Godwin Street, Bradford, in 1990, with its destination already reset for its return journey to Bingley.

Leaving Tyersal on tendered route 66 to Leeds on 29 October 1988 is PMT Cityline's Alexander-bodied Renault S56 No. 528 (E528 JRE).

Seen surprisingly at Tyersal, Bradford, on route 66 to Leeds in March 1996 is GHA Coaches of Wrexham's Marshall-bodied Mercedes-Benz 709D M115 XLV, which was new to Dalybus, Eccles.

Approaching Undercliffe on its way from Otley to Bradford via Leeds Bradford Airport is Rhodes Coaches of Yeadon's Plaxton-bodied Leyland Leopard 26 BMR, which is displaying its destination on a board in its windscreen.

About to be overtaken by a West Yorkshire Road Car Co. Leyland National 2 in Bradford Interchange is a Rhodes Coaches of Yeadon's ex-London Country Leyland National (NPD 143L), which was collecting its Leeds Bradford Airport passengers.

Seen in Halifax bus station awaiting its departure to Bradford on route 682 is Roe-bodied Leyland Olympian No. 5111 (A111 KUM), with lettering publicising the fact that its owner, Yorkshire Rider, had been purchased from West Yorkshire PTE by its employees. (Author's collection)

Bradford Buses

Painted in the pre-war Bradford Corporation livery is Yorkshire Rider's Roe-bodied Leyland Olympian No. 5040 (CUB 40Y), which is seen here in Bridge Street, Bradford.

Wearing West Yorkshire Road Car Co. heritage livery, Yorkshire Rider's ECW-bodied Leyland Olympian No. 5199 (C485 YWY), which was new to the former NBC, leaves Bradford Interchange on a 620 journey to Cottingley.

Continuing the Yorkshire Rider heritage theme, Roe-bodied Leyland Olympian No. 5134 (B134 RWY) is seen here at Thornbury in February 1995 wearing Bradford City Transport's post-war colours.

Still in the livery of its original owner, West Yorkshire Road Car Co., but with Yorkshire Rider vinyls covering its former fleet name, is ECW-bodied Leyland Olympian No. 5193 (FUM 499Y).

Bradford Buses

Passing through Forster Square, Bradford, in January 1988 on the Shop Hopper service is Yorkshire Rider's Optare Star Rider-bodied Mercedes-Benz 811D No. 2001 (E201 PWY).

New to West Yorkshire PTE, No. 8515 (LUG 515P) was one of a pair of Plaxton-bodied Leyland Leopards surprisingly repainted into the livery of the erstwhile West Yorkshire Road Car Co. at the time when that company's buses were being transformed into Yorkshire Rider's colours.

Repainted into Yorkshire Rider livery but given West Yorkshire fleet names, former West Yorkshire Road Car Co. ECW-bodied Bristol VRT No. 744 (LUA 472V) is about to turn into Bradford Interchange from Bridge Street in 1990.

Three former West Yorkshire Road Car Co. buses resting in Bradford Interchange are headed by Leyland National 2 No. 1353 (UWY 75X), which has been repainted into Yorkshire Rider livery with Huddersfield identification.

Bradford Buses

With its Yorkshire Rider fleet name replaced with CalderLine lettering, Alexander-bodied Volvo B10B No. 1030 (L130 PWR) prepares to enter Bradford Interchange from Bridge Street on 10 April 1997.

Having lost its Yorkshire Rider identity in favour of First Leeds City Link lettering, Roe-bodied Leyland AN68A/1R No. 6256 (PUA 256W) leaves Bradford Interchange at the start of its journey back to its home city.

Yorkshire Woollen District's ECW-bodied Leyland Olympian No. 602 (D602 UUM) still wears West Yorkshire PTE corporate livery but with its MetroBus fleet name replaced by 'Yorkshire' in Bradford Interchange, while behind it is similarly clothed West Riding ECW-bodied Bristol VRT No. 857 (XNW 869S).

Approaching Odsal Top from Low Moor on 1 August 1986 is Yorkshire Woollen District's ECW-bodied Bristol VRT No. 910 (RUA 460W), painted in its owner's post-NBC livery.

One of a large number of Leyland Lynx buses operated by Yorkshire Woollen District, freshly repainted No. 272 (F272 AWW) is seen here loading for a journey to Huddersfield.

Adorned with Fastaway branding and displaying a 'Yorkshire Heckmondwike' fleet name on its foremost upper deck side panel, Yorkshire Woollen District ECW-bodied Leyland Olympian No. 614 (C614 ANW) departs from Bradford Interchange on a journey to Sheffield.

Painted in National Express Airlink livery, Yorkshire Woollen District Van Hool-bodied Scania K113CRB No. 56 (M56 AWW) is seen here leaving Bradford Interchange on its long journey to Gatwick in 1987. It was, when only three years old, rebodied by East Lancs as a bus for Yorkshire Traction.

Still wearing NBC corporate poppy-red livery but with its MetroBus fleet name having been replaced by 'Yorkshire Traction', Leyland National 2 No. 247 (NKU 247X) awaits its Huddersfield-bound passengers at Bradford Interchange.

Thandi Coaches of Southall operated a daily journey from Bradford to its home town. Seen here at Bradford Interchange preparing for its south-bound journey is Plaxton-bodied Volvo No. B58 UJY 574V, which had started life with Trathens at Yelverton.

New to Western National, Independent of Horsforth's ECW-bodied Bristol No. RELL6G TUO 257J, seen here in Queensbury, was given an all-over livery for Asda, for whom it operated several free shoppers bus contracts.

Starting life with London Transport, Pride of the Road's Leyland National OJD 901R heads along Reevy Road, Buttershaw, on a 646 journey to Bradford city centre on 1 June 1991.

Seen in Little Horton Lane, Bradford, on its way to the city centre on 13 March 1991, is Pride of the Road's ex-Merthyr Tydfil Wadham Stringer-bodied Dennis Lancet, SDW 237Y.

Pride of the Road competed with Yorkshire Rider on the 646 service from Bradford city centre to Buttershaw, at which terminus its former Barrow Borough Transport Talbot Pullman E658 OCW is seen together with Yorkshire Rider's Roe-bodied Leyland Olympian No. 5142 (B503 RWY) on 1 June 1991.

Bradford Metropolitan District Council operates a large fleet of welfare buses, one of which – Dodge B189 SWU – is seen here in 1988.

Small Bradford independent Emmfield Coaches employed ex-Barrow Borough Transport Leyland National SEO 209M on schools duties. Here it is seen returning to its Great Horton depot on 8 March 1994.

Abundant Life Centre operated a small, albeit varied fleet of buses to transport its worshipers to church and community projects. Seen here at its Bradford base on 7 April 2001 are, from left to right, ECW-bodied Bristol VRT BTU 370S, which was new to Crosville; ex-Greater Manchester PTE NCME-bodied Daimler CRG6LX JVM 993N; former Blackpool Transport Marshall-bodied Dennis Lancet VCW 596Y; Plaxton-bodied Leyland Leopard AAU 136A; ex-Chesterfield Transport Leyland National VKU 71S; and Leyland National MOD 828P, which began life with Western National.

Bradford Buses 43

Approaching Bradford Interchange on 19 June 1990 is Keighley & District's ECW-bodied Bristol VRT No. 306 (DWU 297T), whose previous cream centre band has been repainted grey.

Clothed in Keighley & District's then new grey and red livery, former West Yorkshire Road Car Co. ECW-bodied Leyland Olympian No. 371 (B515 UWW) climbs Bridge Street, Bradford, on its way to the Interchange on 6 August 1990.

Merely having had the green area of its former owner London Country North East's livery repainted red, Keighley & District's ECW-bodied Leyland Olympian No. 376 (B265 LPH) leaves Bradford Interchange on its journey to Keighley and Oxenhope on 6 August 1990.

Wearing Keighley & District's new predominantly white livery, leaving Bradford Interchange is ex-London Country North East ECW-bodied Leyland Olympian No. 974 (B261LPH), upon which 'Keep Tidy' promotional lettering had been added.

Carrying Star Bus branding and route details below its side windows, Keighley & District's Alexander-bodied Volvo B10B No. 503 (N503 HWY) turns from Bridge Street into Bradford Interchange on 27 January 1997.

Wibsey-based minicoach operator Yorkshire Stag purchased a number of Alexander-bodied Leyland AN68C/1Rs via auction that were previously operated by the failed Yorkbus, but which were new to Lothian Buses. They were, however, never used by their new owner and after a long period in store were all sold. Here GSC 625X, GSC 655X and an unidentified example are seen at Yorkshire Stag's depot on 27 March 2000, still wearing their previous owner's livery.

Bradford Traveller's ex-West Yorkshire Road Car Co. Robin Hood-bodied Iveco 49.10 No. 2101 (G211 KUA) with Micro Rider fleet names is followed up Bridge Street, Bradford, by No. 5218 (G618 OWR), one of the company's Alexander-bodied Leyland Olympians.

Wearing Flagship livery, Yorkshire Rider Bradford's Roe-bodied Leyland Olympian No. 5082 (A82 KUM) approaches the Interchange on the 636 service to Clayton in 1994.

Having just departed from Bradford Interchange on 25 May 1996, ex-GM Buses Northern Counties-bodied Leyland AN68A/1R No. 6423 (UNA 800S) carries its new Bradford Traveller fleet name on its former Yorkshire Rider livery.

Displaying their new experimental First Bradford Traveller liveries, Roe-bodied Leyland Olympians No. 5098 (A98 KUM) and No. 5114 (A114 KUM) stand in Nelson Street outside Bradford Interchange at their launch on 14 February 1996.

Another of First Bradford Traveller's trial liveries is seen on Alexander-bodied Leyland Olympian No. 5205 (G605 OWR) as it leaves Bradford Interchange on 5 March 1996.

Yet another of First Bradford Traveller's experimental liveries is shown on Roe-bodied Leyland Olympian No. 5084 as it climbs Moore Avenue en route to Odsal on 19 April 1996.

A further variation of First Bradford Traveller's new colours can be seen on Roe-bodied Leyland AN68/1R No. 6032 (GUG 559N), which is seen here making its way along Reevy Road, Buttershaw, on 21 June 1996.

Leaving Bradford Interchange is First Bradford Travellers' No. 2010 (D539 FAE), one of a number of Dormobile-bodied Mercedes-Benz L608Ds acquired from First Bristol.

Climbing Bridge Street on their way to Bradford Interchange on 10 April 1997 are First Bradford Traveller Plaxton-bodied Mercedes-Benz 709D No. 2268 (N268 JUG) and Alexander-bodied Leyland Olympian No. 5221 (G621 OWR).

Seen leaving Bradford Interchange on the staff shuttle bus service to First Bradford's depot in 1998 is Plaxton-bodied Mercedes-Benz 0814D demonstrator P296 JHE.

Bradford Buses 51

The only Dennis Dominator to be operated by First CalderLine was former First South Yorkshire Alexander-bodied No. 5551 (NKU 207X), which is seen here passing through Ambler Thorn on a 576 journey from Bradford to Halifax on 14 August 2002.

Heading up Bridge Street ready to enter Bradford Interchange on 8 March 1997 is First Kingfisher Plaxton's Verde-bodied Dennis Lance No. 4013 (M613 VWW), which already had its destination blind reset for its journey back to its home base at Huddersfield.

Also seen in Bridge Street, Bradford, nearing the end of its journey from Leeds on 8 March 1997, is First Leeds City Link's Roe-bodied Leyland Olympian No. 5143 (B504 RWY) in its attractive new livery.

Posed at the Carrbottom Road bus stop on the new Manchester Road guided busway during a press preview prior to its opening in October 2001 is First Bradford's Alexander-bodied Volvo B7TL No. 5757 (W757 DWX).

Seen in Cooper Lane, Buttershaw, on 5 August 2000 on the 646 Greengates circular service while being evaluated by First Bradford is Alexander's ALX400-bodied Dennis Trident demonstrator V929 FMS.

Another bus demonstrated to First Bradford, albeit not used in service, Wrightbus-bodied DAF SB120 Electrocity hybrid YG52 CCX is seen here at First Bradford's depot on 5 March 2003 with a couple of Alexander-bodied Leyland Olympians in the background.

Painted in a one-off experimental livery and seen here on driver training duties on 18 August 2001 is First Bradford's Northern Counties-bodied Volvo Olympian No. 5604 (L604 PWR).

Resting at their owner's depot in March 2003, First Bradford's Roe-bodied Leyland Olympians No. 5088 (A88 KUM) and No. 5139 (B139 RWY) both wear First's corporate 'faded' livery and sport school bus logos at each side of their front destination apertures.

Bradford Buses

Leaving Bradford Interchange on a journey to Leeds Bradford Airport on a murky 27 February 1996 is Godson of Leeds' Ikarus-bodied DAF SB220 M764 PWR, which carried branding on its side panels for the service on which it was operating.

For a while Blue Bus, from its local base at Huddersfield, competed with First on the 576 service from Halifax to Bradford. Here, former Rhymney Valley's East Lancs-bodied Leyland Tiger No. 75 (B25 ADW) pauses at Queensbury on 5 March 1996. (Barry Newsome)

Collecting its Shipley-bound passengers in Market Street, Bradford, on 19 January 1996 is Blue Bus's Alexander-bodied Leyland PSU3E/4R ULS3 29T, which started life north of the border with Alexander (Midland).

Followed up Bridge Street on its way to Bradford Interchange by Yorkshire Rider Leeds' Alexander-bodied Scania N113DRB No. 8012 (H612 VNW) is Blue Bus's ex-Rhymney Valley East Lancs-bodied Leyland Tiger No. 73 (A73 VTX) on 19 January 1996.

Operating on its Bradford to Leeds service, for which it has a makeshift destination display, is Amberley of Pudsey's ex-Midland Red Marshall-bodied Leyland PSU3B/2R JHA 217L.

About to enter Bradford Interchange is Black Prince's Alexander-bodied Ailsa B55 SSN 254S, which still wears the livery of Tayside Public Transport Co., from whom it was purchased, and carries route details on its upper side panels for the 88 service, which it had acquired from Amberley Travel.

Much-travelled Alexander-bodied Ailsa B55 JOV 749P started life with West Midlands PTE before passing to London Buses, A1 Service, Ardrossan and then Morley-based Black Prince, with whom it is seen here in Bridge Street, Bradford, on 27 February 1996, still wearing the livery of A1 Service.

Also in Bridge Street, albeit on 23 December 1998, and still wearing its former owner Stagecoach's corporate livery, is Black Prince's Northern Counties-bodied Scania BR112DH, which was new to Greater Manchester PTE.

One of four ex-London AEC Routemasters operated by Halifax Joint Committee, the oldest of which, WLT 324, stands in Bradford Interchange on 8 April 1999 before starting its return journey to Halifax via Queensbury driven by the author.

Competing with First on its service between Bradford and Halifax, and seen at Clayton Heights operating a short working to Queensbury on 11 June 2002, is Halifax Joint Committee's ex-Arriva Leaside MCW Metrobus KYV 793X, which has yet to be repainted.

One of Halifax Joint Committee's short-lived Leyland Nationals, ex-Yorkshire Traction YWG 460T passes through Catherine Slack on its way from Bradford to Halifax on 25 August 2000. Despite being repainted into its new owner's livery, it only remained in service for two months before being sold for scrap.

Heading along Leeds Road, Thornbury, on 15 April 2002 on its twice-daily X72 service from Bradford to Leeds is Halifax Joint Committee's ex-Arriva London North MCW Metrobus GYE 422W.

Leased by Birstall-based Bradford Bus Company from dealers Mistral, Knutsford, and seen here on White Abbey Road, Bradford, on 26 July 2001, Plaxton-bodied Dennis Dart SLF S783 RNE carries its route details on stickers below its side windows.

Also making its way along White Abbey Road on 26 July 2001 is Bradford Bus Company's MCW Metrobus GOG 227W, which began life with West Midlands PTE.

Nearing the end of its journey from Slough and Leicester, Bahrat Travel's Plaxton-bodied Volvo B10M VJI 8687 climbs Bridge Street, Bradford, on 10 November 1998 before turning into the Interchange. New to Grey Green, London, it was originally registered D88 2FYL.

Although exhibited when new at the 1984 Commercial Motor Show in Ebdon of Sidcup livery, coach-seated ECW-bodied Leyland Olympian XSU 913 began life, however, with South Yorkshire PTE, with whom it was registered 4475 WE. Seen here on 12 December 2005 it is owned by Saltaire Travel, who used it on prestigious private hire and party bus duties.

Standing outside its owner's premises at Undercliffe on 12 September 2004 is Wrose Travel's Plaxton-bodied Volvo B10M OIL 5838.

Briefly hired by Wrose Travel from PC Coaches, Lincoln, and seen here in Queensbury operating a local schools service on 21 July 2005, is MCW Metrobus GYE 576W, which was new to London Transport.

A1 Coaches of Shipley's ex-London Park Royal-bodied Daimler CRL6 KUC 181P is seen here at its depot on 7 May 2004 in the company of NCME-bodied Leyland FE30AGR BCS 874T, which began life with Western SMT, and former Northern General's ECW-bodied Leyland AN68A/1R MBR 439T, all of which were employed on school bus duties.

Resting at its depot on 3 March 2004 is A1 Coaches of Shipley's Plaxton-bodied Volvo B10M MUI 5490.

Climbing up Great Horton Road, Bradford, while undertaking a school bus service on 20 April 2004, is Shipley-based A1 Coaches' Alexander-bodied Leyland AN68/1R OVK 149M, which was new to Tyne & Wear PTE.

Seen outside the Alhambra Theatre in Morley Street, Bradford, on 14 September 1991, coach-seated Alexander-bodied Volvo B10M-50 F682 FWX was the first double-decker to be operated by Bradford-based coach operator Dewhirst, who had purchased it new.

Resting at their Shipley depot on 24 April 2009 are Travel Express' East Lancs-bodied Dennis Dominator LUI 9693, which was previously owned by Bournemouth Yellow Buses, with whom it was registered H251 JTT, and Unvi-bodied Mercedes-Benz 0815 minicoach YN06 JFK.

Displaying an Arriva Express fleet name, Wright-bodied Volvo B10B 408 (L408 NUA), seen here in Bridge Street in the pouring rain on 27 January 2000, began life with West Riding, wearing its cream and green livery.

Illustrating three different liveries at Bradford Traveller's depot on 13 November 1998 are, from left to right: ex-First Manchester Wright-bodied Volvo B10BLE No. 1049 (S668 RNA) and Wright-bodied Scania L113CRL No. 8446 (S446 BSG), both of which are wearing corporate 'barbie' colours; ex-First Manchester Northern Counties-bodied Leyland AN68A/1R No. 6442 (FVR 266V) in Bradford Traveller livery; and Roe-bodied Leyland AN68A/1R No. 6203 (JUM 203V) still in Yorkshire Rider's cream and green.

Being demonstrated at the Cedar Hotel, Rooley Lane, Bradford, to First Bradford and a local school on 8 September 2000, is an unregistered, American-built Bluebird AARE yellow school bus with First logos.

Leaving Bradford Interchange on a journey to Leeds Bradford Airport is Aztecbird of Guiseley's long-wheelbase Optare Solo YJ54 BVA, which was leased from West Yorkshire PTE and painted in its MetroConnect livery with discreet 737 route branding.

Collecting its passengers in Nelson Street outside Bradford Interchange on 24 July 2000 is First Bradford's three-week-old Wright-bodied Volvo B7LA bendy bus No. 1123 (W128 DWX), which carries branding for routes 617 and 618 on the cover panels of its front module and sports a 'Sovereign' name below its cabside window. After a comparatively short life in Bradford it was transferred to First York for use on its Park and Ride services, before moving to First Leeds where it was to ultimately end its life.

Travelling down Harrogate Road, Rawdon, on its way from Leeds Bradford Airport on 3 June 2002 is First Bradford Optare Solo No. 2317 (W317 DWX), which has 'Sovereign' branding at the base of the window above its rear wheel arch.

Seen on 27 January 2004, while being demonstrated to First Bradford, is Wrightbus-bodied Dennis Dart SLF Electrocity hybrid AKZ 7122. In the event, however, it was not used in revenue-earning service during its brief visit.

Awaiting time in Queensbury on 5 February 2005 while operating the Lime Line 576 service from Halifax to Bradford, for which it was heavily branded, is First Halifax's one-month-old Wright-bodied Volvo B7TL No. 32527 (YJ54 XUU).

Leaving First Bradford's depot on 9 March 2005 to take up its duties on a works service is Alexander-bodied Volvo B7TL No. 30878 (W733 DWX), which carries route branding above its lower-deck side windows and 'Overground' lettering between its wheel arches.

Evaluated by First Bradford for several months and largely used on the 607 service from Thornton to Holme Wood, Temsa Avenue, No. 63000 (YJ10 BVA) is seen here on Thornton Road on 27 July 2010. After returning to dealer Arriva DAF at Gomersal at the end of its trial, it was ultimately sold to Arriva North East.

Wearing Transdev Keighley & District's original 'Shuttle' livery for the 662 service from Keighley to Bradford, Wright-bodied Volvo B7RLE No. 1801 (YJ05 FNP) heads along Manningham Lane, Bradford, on 20 April 2010.

New to Transdev Lancashire United and transferred to Transdev Keighley & District in 2014, Wright-bodied Volvo B7RLE No. 1825 (YJ07 PBX) approaches Bradford Interchange on 23 October 2014 while clothed in the second variation of 'Shuttle' branding.

In 2015, Transdev Keighley & District refurbished a number of its 2005 Wright-bodied Volvo B7RLEs, re-registered them, and painted them in yet another new livery for 'Shuttle' service 662. Here No. 1801 (SNZ 801), which was originally registered YJ05 FNP, leaves Bradford Interchange on 4 April 2017 en route to Keighley.

Transdev Keighley & District Wright-bodied Volvo B10BLE No. 543 (T543 AUA) stands at the bottom of Sunbridge Road, Bradford, on its way to the Interchange on 2 April 2008.

Heading up Bridge Street, Bradford, on its way to the Interchange on 4 April 2017, and displaying its new Keighley Bus Company fleet name on its front panel, is Wright-bodied Volvo B10BLE No. 1079 (PO51 MTE), which was new to Lancashire United in November 2001.

Much-travelled Plaxton President-bodied Volvo B7TL No. 2711 (Y711 HRN) began life in 2001 with Transdev Burnley & Pendle and then ran for Yorkshire Coastliner, Harrogate & District and Lancashire United before joining Transdev Keighley & District in 2011. Here it is seen approaching Bradford Interchange on 7 October 2015.

Leaving Bradford Interchange on the West Yorkshire PTE-tendered 846 service to Buttershaw on 4 April 2017 is Keighley Bus Company's Plaxton-bodied Dennis Dart MPD No. 703 (YG52 GDJ), which has been painted into a promotional livery for App Tap fare payment. New to Harrogate & District it has also operated with Burnley & Pendle (twice), Lancashire United and then Harrogate & District again before joining the Keighley fleet in 2016.

Wearing an anonymous cream livery with Transdev fleet names, Keighley Bus Company's Transbus Dart MPD No. 719 (YJ04 LYD) is seen in Bradford Interchange on 4 April 2017 on the West Yorkshire PTE-tendered 847 service to Wibsey. New to Keighley & District, it has since seen service with Burnley & Pendle, Lancashire United and Yorkshire Coastliner before returning to its original home in 2015.

Painted in a dedicated livery for the X6 Huddersfield to Leeds service, but yet to receive its graphics, First Bradford's Wright-bodied Volvo B7TL No. 37060 (YJ06 XMM) is seen leaving Bradford Interchange on 17 February 2007.

Trialled by First Bradford on the Shop Hopper service, battery-powered Minitram VO52 AFA climbs Bridge Street on its way to the Interchange on 4 October 2005 – its first day in operation – followed by First Bradford's Alexander-bodied Volvo B7TL No. 30872 (W727 DWX).

Seen on 28 April 2010 at the temporary interchange at St Ives, Bingley, during a protracted road closure is local independent Mikes Travel's Renault Excel YN51 YTM, which was on hire to First Bradford for the operation of a shuttle service to Bingley. Behind it, ready to return to Bradford, is First Bradford's Wright-bodied Volvo B7L No. 60924 (YG02 DHE), which began life with First York.

One of twenty-six Wright-bodied Volvo B7LA 'FTR' bendy buses refurbished and given Hyperlink branding for the 72 service, No. 19004 (MH06 ZSW), which was new to First York and registered B7 FTR, makes its way along Nelson Street, Bradford, on its way from Leeds to the Interchange on 6 February 2014.

Sandwiched between Wright-bodied Volvo B7LA 'FTR' bendy buses Nos. 19020 (YJ07 LVM) and 19022 (YJ07 LVO) – both of which, not having been part of the Hyperlink refurbishment programme, were stored in their original livery at First Bradford's depot on 7 August 2014 – is Alexander-bodied Volvo Olympian No. 31768 (R932 YOV), which had begun life with London United.

Branded for the Leeds to Bradford 72 service, First Bradford's Wright-bodied Volvo B9TL No. 37065 (YK57 EZU) turns into Bradford Interchange on 24 July 2009.

About to turn into Leeds Bradford Airport while on a private hire duty on 26 April 2010 is CT Plus (Yorkshire) BMC No. 220 YJ56 ZTF, which was leased from West Yorkshire PTE and wears the original My Bus livery with maroon skirt.

Having been repainted into a green livery for its demonstration to First West Yorkshire, Wright-bodied 'New Bus for London' LT61 BHT, which eventually returned to Arriva London North, is seen here being examined at First Bradford's depot on 7 August 2014.

Wrightbus StreetLite's DF demonstrator DRZ 9713, painted in First Potteries livery and given fleet number 63160, is seen here as it climbs Bridge Street, Bradford, on 7 October 2015 while on loan to First Bradford.

Repainted into pseudo Halifax Corporation heritage livery, First Halifax's Wright-bodied Volvo B7TL No. 37048 (YJ06 XLY) passes through Clayton Heights on the 576 service from Bradford to Halifax on 1 May 2015.

Another heritage livery is that of West Yorkshire Road Car Co., which was given to First Leeds' Wright-bodied Volvo B9TL No. 37675 (YJ58 RTX), which is seen here on 19 April 2016 displaying former West Yorkshire Leyland Olympian fleet number 1812 on its front panel.

Looking superb in its erstwhile Bradford City Transport heritage livery, First Bradford's Wright-bodied Volvo B9TL No. 37732 (YJ09 OCD) makes its way up Bridge Street, Bradford, on 4 April 2017.

Painted in First Group's new corporate livery and sporting striped lower front corner panels, First Bradford's Wright-bodied Volvo B7RLE No. 69573 (BD13 OHN), seen here leaving Bradford Interchange on 4 April 2017, started life with First Manchester.

Another bus with striped front corner panels, First Bradford's Wrightbus StreetLite DF No. 63278 (SL15 ZFH) leaves Bradford Interchange on an X11 journey to Leeds on 4 April 2017.

Wearing a dedicated livery for the frequent express X6 service to Leeds, First Bradford's Wrightbus StreetDeck No. 35237 (SL16 YPA) is seen leaving Bradford Interchange on 4 April 2017.

Bradford Buses

Repainted into a dedicated livery for the limited-stop X63 service to Huddersfield is First Bradford's Wright-bodied Volvo B9TL No. 37086 (YJ08 GVY), which is pictured here entering Nelson Street, Bradford, from the Interchange on 4 April 2017.

One of the vehicles that replaced the 'FTR' Hyperlink bendy buses on the Bradford to Leeds 72 service, First Leeds' Wrightbus StreetDeck No. 35216 (SL16 RGU) makes its way up Nelson Street before entering Bradford Interchange on 4 April 2017.

Departing from Bradford Interchange is Arriva Yorkshire's Optare Spectra-bodied DAF DB250 No. 704 (JG52 CFA).

Branded for the 268 service and displaying route details and 'Connecting Kirklees' lettering on its lower side panels, Arriva Yorkshire's Alexander Dennis Enviro400 Trident No. 1911 (YJ58 FHN) turns into Bradford Interchange from Nelson Street on 6 February 2014.

Heading down Bridge Street to Bradford Interchange on 7 October 2015 is Arriva Yorkshire's Alexander Dennis Enviro200 No. 1054 (YJ09 CTZ).

Caught by the camera leaving Bradford Interchange on 23 October 2014, Arriva Yorkshire's Alexander Dennis Enviro400 Trident No. 1902 is repainted into then-new Max livery and branded for route 268.

Seen in Bradford Interchange on 6 February 2014 while operating the 711 service is Geldards of Leeds' Alexander-bodied Dennis Trident No. 366 (KV02 USP), which began life in London with Connex.

Hull-based Stagecoach's Plaxton-bodied Volvo B12B No. 53030 (YU04 YAG), seen here in Nelson Street preparing to turn into Bradford Interchange on 14 November 2012, carries MegabusPlus fleet names for its service to London, upon which passengers change at East Midlands Parkway station onto a Stagecoach East Midlands train in order to complete their journey to the capital.

Wearing National Express livery and heading down Bridge Street to Bradford Interchange on its way from Middlesbrough to Liverpool is Go-Northern Caetano-bodied Scania K340EB6 No. 7102 (FJ08 KNW) on 23 October 2014.

Since it acquired Bradford independent coach-operator Feather Brothers in the 1950s, Wallace Arnold has undertaken some of the city's coach operations. Seen here is R416 FWT, one of its once-large fleet of Plaxton-bodied Volvo B10Ms. (T.W.W. Knowles)

Displaying Leeds Bradford Airport Direct branding and seen leaving the airport on service 747 to Bradford on 26 April 2010 is Centrebus Scania CN94UB Omnicity No. 786 (YN03 UWS), which started life with Menzies at Heathrow and in whose livery it is still painted.

Centrebus rarely employed double-deckers on its services to Leeds Bradford Airport but on 26 April 2010 former London United East Lancs-bodied Scania N230UD No. 906 (YN07 LHZ) is seen approaching the air terminal at the end of its journey from Bradford.

Bradford Buses

New to Huddersfield Bus Company, Yorkshire Tiger's Optare Tempo No. 773 (YJ10 EZF) turns from Bridge Street into Bradford Interchange at the end of its journey from Leeds Bradford Airport on 7 October 2015.

Although Yorkshire Tiger Optare Versa No. 791 (YJ14 BWV), seen here at Leeds Bradford Airport on 27 April 2014 for the launch of the Flying Tiger-branded services, displays Leeds service 757 on its destination screen, these buses also operate the 737 and 747 services, which connect the airport to Bradford, as do Flying Tiger-branded Scania Omnicitys.

Photographed through the window of Bradford Interchange, which unfortunately caused reflections, Yorkshire Tiger's ex-Ipswich Buses Optare Solo No. 300 (YN03 NDU) was caught unusually operating route 737 to Leeds Bradford Airport on 4 April 2017.

Painted in West Yorkshire PTE's MetroConnect livery, Bradford-based TLC's Optare Solo MX54 KXV travels on route MC3 along Horton Park Avenue, Bradford, on 15 March 2005, which served both a Tesco and a Morrison's supermarket.

Wearing West Yorkshire PTE Access Bus livery, TLC of Bradford's slim-line Optare Solo No. 3387 (YJ09 KZR) stands on the car park of Morrison's supermarket, Rooley Lane, Bradford, on 24 August 2015.

About to turn from Bridge Street into Bradford Interchange on 7 October 2015 is TLC Travel of Bradford's Alexander Dennis E20D No. 13972 (YY64 TXU) followed by First Bradford Wright-bodied Volvo B7RLE No. 69321 (YJ09 FWR).

Heading to Otley on the tendered 653 service from Bradford on 22 July 2009 is TLC Travel's MetroConnect-branded slim-line Optare Solo 1542 (MX54 KYK), which began life with Stringers of Pontefract.

Passing through Northowram while not on service on 2 August 2015 is TLC's slim-line Optare Solo No. 90815 (YD63 VEB), whose fleet number matches its chassis number, as is customary in this operator's fleet.

One of a large fleet of low-floor BMC 220 school buses owned by West Yorkshire PTE, No. 68628 (YJ06 WTV), which is leased to First Bradford, shows off its revised livery with lime green skirt as it turns into Bradford Interchange on 7 October 2015.

Travelling down Morley Street on 19 May 2016 while operating the Bradford City Bus service is Brighouse-based Ladies Only Travel's Optare Solo No. Ladies 11 (R90 LOT), which was new to First West Yorkshire registered YJ58CDY.

City Travel of Cullingworth – whose Van Hool-bodied DAF MB230 XIL 7877 is seen here in April 2009 – operate a number of tendered school bus services around the Bradford area, including a number of BMC 220s painted in My Bus livery and leased from West Yorkshire PTE.

Seen on 24 April 2010 providing the free shuttle service between the terminal building and long stay car park is Leeds Bradford Airport's Optare Solo YJ07 EHS, which was one of a pair bought new in 2007.

One of three ex-Stagecoach London Mercedes-Benz 0530G bendy buses purchased by Leeds Bradford Airport in 2014 for airside use, internally registered BUS 42 retains its former operator's livery, onto which LBA logos have been added. (Leeds Bradford Airport)

New to Central Parking at Luton Airport and later used at Gatwick airport before being acquired by Leeds Bradford Airport, Transbus Dart SLF KX53 SFO is seen here operating the free shuttle service between the terminal building and long stay car park at its new home on 23 October 2014.

Approaching Bradford Interchange on 19 April 2016 at the end of its journey from Leeds Bradford Airport is Yorkshire Tiger's ex-Menzies, Heathrow Scania Omnicity No. 784 (YN03 UWP), which wears dedicated Flying Tiger branding.

Looking immaculate as it stands between duties at Bradford Interchange on 4 April 2017 is recently acquired and freshly repainted First Bradford's Alexander-bodied Volvo B7TL No. 32091 (KP51 WCJ), which began life with First Leicester.